Home
Confessions

Salyers'
the love, memories,
and words of encouragement
are my fuel. What fun we
have and may it never stop!
Love,
Kellie

Home
Confessions

KELLIE WRIGHT

TATE PUBLISHING
AND ENTERPRISES, LLC

Published by Tate Publishing & Enterprises, LLC
127 E. Trade Center Terrace | Mustang, Oklahoma 73064 USA
1.888.361.9473 | www.tatepublishing.com

Tate Publishing is committed to excellence in the publishing industry. The company reflects the philosophy established by the founders, based on Psalm 68:11,
"The Lord gave the word and great was the company of those who published it."

Book design copyright © 2016 by Tate Publishing, LLC. All rights reserved.
Cover design by Bill Francis Peralta
Interior design by Jomar Ouano

Published in the United States of America

ISBN: 978-1-68164-763-0
1. Biography & Autobiography / Personal Memoirs
2. Biography & Autobiography / Women
16.04.11

Toddlers in a Craft Store

In my perfect world, I have no budget when it comes to the big HL. No matter your views on this particular store, there is no denying the endless decor and craft potential this store has. Today the pilgrimage was due to the fact that we have an exciting wedding coming up, and there isn't a bouquet ready, not a vase filled, and not a single trip to Hobby Lobby made this month! It is the *fourth* day of October after all. So we had to check off these boxes and make the hour-long car ride to the nearest holy land—I mean, Hobby Lobby.

This trip would consist of my lovely mother-in-law, my two-and-a-half-year-old son, and my eleventh-month-old son. It was guaranteed to go smoothly! Now, normally, the company of my babies is an immediate red flag for any store that has breakables; but we had two drivers (of shopping carts), and we had two kids. Therefore, our odds were pretty good. My mother-in-law, having four kids under ten at one time, is a well-seasoned champ at the "kids in public acting like they don't want to be on the same planet as anyone else" routine. We had the snacks in purse, sippies filled, eyeliner and mascara applied, and we were out the door.

The trip up there was great. It was an awesome time for me and my MIL to chat while the boys enjoyed watching LeapFrog DVD (educational fun!). When we arrived, she grabbed one boy, and I grabbed the other, and we informed them there are only two ways to approach this future outing when they are older.

1. You love this place with every fiber of your being, which you will brag to your fellow masculine deer-hunting, truck-driving buddies about the fun times you enjoy going to Hobby Lobby with your amazing mom *or*—
2. Stay home with Daddy.

I think they understood perfectly.

So we got our minicarts, which were 2 percent the space of a standard grocery-store cart, and took a deep breath as we took in the wonderful panoramic view we were giving ourselves of the happiest place on earth. (In the decorating world, I am totally a Disney fan, so hold the reins if you thought I was pushing the big DL to the side—no, sir.)

We did a great deal of shopping through the store, and the kiddos were really great. The eldest would occasionally see something he knew and would let me know every time we passed a pumpkin. Then he made me have a great mommy moment of feeling my kid would be totally going to college on academic scholarship. Then, as an hour rolled by and we were trying to make the ever-important decision of which candle combination to use, the two-and-and-half-year-old started wanting to escape (a trait I apparently passed down) from the cart. Twenty minutes later, he and I were standing outside the store having a "talk" about how his behavior, yelling, going completely limp, and turning into deadweight while I was trying to carry him wasn't good. I naturally got the NO a few times and he telling me in his own language about how this was all legitimate behavior. He doesn't know that I have already pulled all of this with my folks over two decades ago, and I have more practice at the stubborn thing. So after I let him vent and told him that we get to go eat chicken after we went back inside for just a short while, he hung his head then looked up and wrapped his arms around my neck in a full-on embrace of love and a don't-let-me-go-ever hug.

Toddlers can be awesomely strange.

We checked out. My toddler found great joy in pushing his brother in the minicart by himself to the car, and my MIL and I celebrated the joy in all the savings we just made at the glorious place.

So after all the challenges of little ones, a few stares, and a couple of "why didn't we shop online" thoughts, was it worth it?

Absolutely!

We shall return!

Sometimes, the Fridge Just Wants to Be Cleaned

Today, being Thursday and the very busy seventy-two hours that the hubs and I have ahead of us, I was very excited to have a whole day to stay home and get things accomplished. We had a wedding, possible engagement photos to shoot, a separate wedding shower, and activities at church between tomorrow and Sunday night. So my plan was to stay home, get everything gathered, washed, organized, whatever it may need, to make all this happen as smoothly as possible!

So I woke up (personal pat on the back). I made my amazing cup of happy and drank said cup and started my day.

Nothing big going on. Made the boys some toast and some cereal, but then my oldest decided to take a trip to the fridge. Nothing new. Nothing out of the ordinary, but he also found that the orange juice was just low enough he could lift it and *open* it! I saw this and didn't sweat it because he was just trying to drink from the jug.

No idea on earth where he had learned this from because I have hidden this habit that I have (step one is the hardest) from my children like a pro. However, the rule that I will enforce when they are older is they *must* finish it if they decide to do such a thing.

So I kept watching him, and I saw the look on his face as he took a breath. He examined the remaining orange juice, and the toddler brain started to work. He poured it out. Now this act, I wasn't mad at. I understand that they like to pour; it's in their wiring that they can't help. The part I was a little perturbed about was 1) I was planning on using that OJ to mix with the last can of Squirt to make the best combo drink for myself later and 2) there was a mess. Now, given the proper age, we use natural consequences to teach in our house, so I handed him a towel and instructed him to clean it up. This was nothing new. He knew the drill and went to work. I then finished it up so it wouldn't stick to my feet later, and then all was well.

Then later happened.

Later I was in the living room, which is open to the kitchen, and so I could hear whatever was going on in the kitchen. But the height of our bar and the height of my son make for an invisible toddler to roam in the kitchen and do as he pleases with the stealth of Violet from *The Incredibles* (just no force fields). That is until we *hear* him. Curly ends up at his posting station, inside the fridge; and he is, as usual, sniffing for something to consume.

Breaking news—we do feed our children every day. They eat breakfast, morning snack, lunch, afternoon snack, and dinner. Now we return you to your regular programming.

As I heard him shuffling things in the fridge, I then heard a splattering sound.

NOT GOOD EVER!

I threw down whatever halfway-folded towel that previously had my attention and rounded the corner of the bar to see that my curly-haired almost three-year-old son (sniff) had poured out a half-gallon jug onto the floor. Now we know there was no more orange juice because I already shed a tear over the possibility of enjoying my orange-juice-and-Squirt combo being gone. No, no, no, my sweet angel had found the half gallon, which was down to maybe a fourth of a gallon, of *buttermilk*! Which, by the way, was expired.

Let's take a moment to think about an expired item that has been in your fridge. You need to throw it away, but because it stinks, you want to time this well so it's doesn't stink out of where it is and smell up the house. So it tends to get pushed to the side then to the back and somehow blends in with the back wall of the fridge.

So when I say expired, we are talking almost a month! Yeah, bad! On the plus side, it was buttermilk. It's halfway to yogurt when it's "fresh." I did say, "It poured," not "rolled out of the jug"—it poured.

I scooted the accused out of the kitchen, put my smell blocker over my nose (my T-shirt), and grab a towel. Seeing that is had gone under the fridge, I adjusted my Eskimo Joe pants and prepared to move the fridge to clean out from under it. (Why did I open this can of worms!)

Considering the graphic nature of the condition of the floor under the fridge, we will just skip to the new status of the floor.

Clean! All better! And I found five alphabet magnets.

So now that my toddler had helped me clean out the fridge and under it, I planned on enjoying more coffee than I originally intended and hopefully cross off the list of the eighty-five million things that needed to happen this weekend. If anything else, I could say the fridge was cleaned out!

The Dirt Is Not Gone with the Wind

You know, life is funny and how one day you are just walking along and then—*bam!*—an epiphany slams you between the eyes. Often this comes to me, making me ask myself, *Why didn't I see this before?*

Do you like to watch people in other environments that are not similar to your own? I find that what images of homelife I am interested in watching are *nothing* like mine. It's not to say I don't love mine. I find ours fun and unique, and frankly, I couldn't imagine any other way to live. I like to watch people in their homes, which tend to be pretty shiny homes with a really nice kitchen and clean floors. It's a faraway world to me, so it's almost like a documentary-watching mind-set—you are there to see why they do, what they do.

Thinking about my own homelife in about two and a half years of my marriage, I wondered why there was always dirt on the floor. It's not that I didn't sweep. It's not that it was the same dirt that I swept up yesterday—but why is there so much dirt *inside* the house? Then, when watching one of the pretty shows of "real" people in their shiny kitchens, I saw it. There was my clue. It was headed straight for the place the unibrow tries to grow.

A woman's husband came in from work, and she gave him a hug. He was in a button-down shirt, slacks, and he looked nice. This seemed odd to me, but why? No big deal he was dressed that way. I've seen men dressed like that in real life before.

Bam!

He was coming home from work, and he had no dirt, stains, or unique odor to him. That was it—there was my answer. It all made sense now!

I grew up, and my father left the house in the mornings dressed in clean clothes. He came home with dirt, oil, and—chances are—a stain or two from the work that he did.

They do say you marry a man like your father. I have found many similarities between my father and husband while clearly seeing they are not the same man.

However, one thing I never looked for in a spouse I have had delivered into my home, and I realized that not everyone has this as a regular part of their life. My husband wears work boots, jeans, and long-sleeve shirts to work—

every day. He comes home, and everything that was clean that morning is now dirty. So he has to change all that clothing, and it goes into the laundry room every day. He goes to work five days a week.

Sidenote—invest in a good washer-and-dryer set if this is a similar setting in your home. You know what? Invest in a good washer-and-dryer set even if this is not a similar setting in your home.

So normal to me is this precious dirt on the floor. Normal is that my husband comes home with dirt, creosote, and sweat in his clothes and a smile on his face. I heard in a movie—and I think it helps that Morgan Freeman said it—that "some of the happiest people in the world come home from work smelling to high heaven."

What may be a foreign world to some is every day to others. It's about the contentment in your world that gives you the joy to keep the ball rolling.

Let Me Tell You a Story of a Storm Widow

In my life, there is a season that has been one of great challenge and reward. I am a lineman's wife. If you are like myself (circa 2006) and do not know what linemen are, they are the men and women who work on the power lines and keep our power goin'. Part of the fun of this profession is that people enjoy having electricity all year round! Especially in the cold months where ice storms come into our part of the country with a vengeance! In which I say—"'Tis the season!"

Now, how the run-of-the-mill storm scenario comes about is usually something along these lines:

There is this *devastating* low-pressure system making its way through the United States, and it will be coming in our direction. This is what the meteorologists say anyway. Then before we know it, rain, sleet, ice—oh my! My husband goes to work in the cold when he hears it's his turn to go work in the cold elsewhere. He comes home to pack a bag (the first storm we don't have one ready, but after that, we usually have one packed, ready to go) and gather some last hugs and kisses before heading out the door to go give the people what they need.

When I say "need," I'm not fooling. He has had everything from girls bringing him hot chocolate to a marriage proposal by a sweet eighty-year-old woman when working away on storms. It's precious.

But here at the house was the mother of his children, who had not worn anything but her pajamas in the last week (it is the holidays after all), with her hair in somewhat of a ponytail and whatever part of the banana that the youngest decided he didn't want rubbed on her black sweatshirt. How he could manage to leave is beyond me.

So when he goes, we are always sad to see him go. He is everything to us. My oldest best buddy, my youngest wrestling partner, his wife's fire starter! I mean, literally, he is the only one who can build a fire in our woodburning stove. *But* as the mob wife said, "This is the life I have chosen," so we must press on!

I try to use this time to my advantage when I can. I think of all the Pinterest projects I will do once I clean my house top to bottom—leaving no detail unchecked, including what's under the fridge, of course! Everything shall be sparkling clean. The fridge and pantry will be stocked; and of course, when he walks in the door, a beautiful batch of chocolate-chip cookies will be waiting for him to enjoy while he tells us the tales of his tiring journey. I sell myself this story every time!

Life is funny. You have a plan; then the plan has a backup plan. Somehow life happens—you know, toddlers?

Fast-forward to nap time, during which the eldest decided that his body in no way required rest today; he could manage. I put the youngest down for a nap with ease, bless his gentle heart. *So* I focused my energy on my eldest once more, reminding him of what he was supposed to be doing at this time of the day. Point made, I walked out of the room. I put on a movie that had a story line with no cartoon characters in sight. I brewed a cup of hot tea and scooped some cream in a bowl. It had pecans, so it was healthy, and I rested under a big fuzzy blanket. No kid noises were to be heard, but a thumping sound was.

I walked to my children's room, where the youngest was sleeping, to find my eldest trying to crawl into his crib!

Nooooo!

Don't wake the baby.

Do *not* wake the baby.

Please do not let the baby wake up!

With one swift mommy motion, my eldest was back on his bed, protesting against the current location he was put into. I turned to gaze into the crib where the obedient baby was once sleeping and saw him looking up at me with his lip pouted out, wondering why he was awake. I picked him up, letting him know he was okay and that it would be an awesome idea if he went back to dreamland so Mommy could go enjoy her healthy snack of tea and ice cream. He decided to let out the cry that said he was awake and he had slept just long enough not to go back to sleep.

I spun on a dime to walk out of the room, holding the youngest while making sure the eldest—who had not moved because it was apparently his turn to be the obedient child—was still in his bed. After ten minutes of trying to be a Johnson & Johnson mom by rocking and smiling at my youngest, I came to the conclusion that my restful mommy moment was not going to happen. I turned off my movie, licked the ice-cream bowl clean—in the classiest way, of course—and figured what better time than now to take down the Christmas tree, pack away the toy train, and put away the Christmas decorations.

If storm season has taught me anything, it would be this: You will have many chances to do nothing (like when your power goes out), but you are not guaranteed the time to do what you want, so try to do something. That way, you can say you have accomplished a task for the day.

Tomorrow holds another chance and more ice cream!

Turkeys and Ticks

Have I ever mentioned that we hunt? No? Well, we do. Truthfully I think you could find something to hunt almost every month of the year. Did you know there was a raccoon season? Yes, well, right now, Spring Turkey season is going on. Depending on where you live in the state depends on how long your season is—no matter the game you are hunting; and so by region, you are given a certain amount of days to hunt. This ensures the population will be managed and, at the same time, not killed out.

Where we live, our season does not start until this week. However, where my father's land is (sorry to sound so formal by saying *father*. I have been watching *Downton Abbey* a lot, and it has rubbed off. I would also like to have my breakfast in bed because that is a married woman's right as well! Yeah, such is life), there is a longer season. So trying to put more meat in the freezer and enjoy some organic turkey with the price of fifty cents per shell versus…well actually, I don't think I have ever bought whole turkey breasts, nor seen it ground up; but either way, I know it's more than fifty cents, so when it comes down to it, it was an economical decision!

In turkey hunting, there can be the approach of "just go out in the morning and hunt," or a two-part approach that requires an evening before, and then waking up *really* early the next morning and then go out to hunt.

I am married to a die-hard hunter, so guess which approach we went for?

When you go out the evening before, it's called putting them to bed. This is where you are calling to see where they will roost for the night. Did you know turkeys sleep in trees? Yep, had no clue myself until a couple years ago. Being in the school of *hunting* life, I am a student who will never graduate.

So once we know where they are going to be sleeping their sweet dreams at, we more or less know where to return to the next morning to seek the best results. *Ideally.*

We went out to where we were thinking was a good place to set up and get ready. Getting out of the car to get all covered up (literally head to toe covered. Turkeys have amazing sight, and anything from the color of your skin to blue jeans will send them off in a hurry), the hubs start to use the call a bit to see if any of our pheasant friends were nearby. We used a hen call (the female's voice, it sounds somewhat like a chirp) so the toms (what they call the grown male turkeys, and what is allowed to be hunted in the spring) would call back. Sure enough, one was off less than a half mile or so. We quickly put on our head coverings and caps when I realized I didn't bring gloves. (Make special note to add lightweight camouflage gloves to my hunting wardrobe come spring sale at Bass Pro Shops.)

This is where my devotion to that die-hard hunter comes in. He can walk and walk and walk and walk—because he has this thirst that cannot be quenched, and once he has a thirst for hunting, well, all else has been forgotten, including his wife's poor feet!

He is smart—that man of mine. He knows if he says right off the bat, "Let's just walk for a minute to see where some game might be."

This might even sound like quality time, where a married couple could stroll along and see what they might see. However, they are both carrying shotguns, and the little lady is wearing knee-high snake boots that are not quite broken in because she only wears them twice a year.

"Okay," I say.

We walk for around 5,693 miles before coming to this place.

Nice view of the creek, right?

That is where we needed to go. Up that open hill right in the clearing of those tress.

Yeah, after dropping down twenty-five feet—

Down this path. Yeah, I was carrying Martha (the decoy), my shotgun, a turkey call, and my phone. Naturally, all of this was not going to make it down this hill in one piece, in which I had to throw down something. Guns are expensive, Martha is inflatable. That's her on the bank waiting for me.

I made it! I literally went in to snowboarding mode (where you lean back ever so slightly so you do not go full speed ahead down a steep hill) and walked with my heels down my toes up and very gracefully clomped down that muddy hill. I had my call and my phone in my pocket, so every time I stepped down, my pocket would chirp.

Step, chirp. Step, chirp. Step, chirp.

Graceful.

Here is my guide, and he is quite easy to follow. I just stare. He's very considerate to stop every now and then to call toward the turkey. This gives me a chance to catch up, but I know he's just wanting me to be close to him. This is what I tell myself to keep me going: try to make a rugged hunting trip into a romantic getaway. I try.

Pretty tree.

The sun was starting to set.

But it was just enough light left in the day to check out some other places just in case their might be another tom on the place.

We sat quickly under some trees after setting up Martha, our hen decoy. By the way, we name our decoys for no other reason than to amuse ourselves. It adds absolutely nothing in our favor to hit our target or take home meat. We are just twisted that way.

So this is taken from how I was lying. We heard the toms not far off, so we thought, maybe, since it was not too far, that we would have a chance to lure one out of the thicket.

This little tree was perfect for resting the shotgun on. It's like God planted this little baby for hunters. It's hard to see Martha out beyond the grass, but she's out there.

After finding the tom we were hearing earlier was still the same distance away, and that I apparently was lying on top of the local tick colony, we figured the turkeys were down for the night.

To be frank here, turkeys are like any wild animal, and they have three priorities in life: eating, sleeping, pursuing. That's about it. So if we, as humans, are trying to lure them anywhere, we need to figure out what will make them move. Except, turkeys really must like sleep, because they will not go very far, if at all, to move toward one of the opposite sex. I am certain if this tom laid eyes on Martha, then his mind would have been forever changed; however, the bum thought *she* could come to him if she was interested.

That being said, we decided that it was good to know that much as to their location and head home.

The next morning, we returned a little before daylight with our ambition set. We also brought Martha back to raise her self-confidence and assured her that we were planning on killing the dumb tom since he thought he was some struttin' turkey who would not give her a chance. We care like that. We also brought along some new friends. We had purchased another hen decoy—Louisa. Also a tom decoy—Larry.

The hubs and I split up to try to find different toms that would be far enough apart where we would not be calling the same tom. I grabbed Martha, and the hubs grabbed Larry and Louisa. Starting on my path, I decided to venture a little farther down the path past the tick colony and keep my path going toward a tom I was hearing farther out. When I found my covered spot and Martha her open area, I was all set.

Waiting, waiting, waiting; it's a killer. If you are able to hear the tom you are calling, it's exciting because their gobble will keep you motivated to wait some more, but eventually they will hush and come in. Unfortunately, he just dropped off completely. No sign of him at all for some time. Although I wasn't crazy about walking, I decided to move toward the cedar pond to see if I could catch them coming in for a drink.

No luck. Got a nap in, but no turkeys.

After taking my call and gun to the car, I unloaded my shells and made my way to where the hubs was across the way, to see if he had any luck, in which he informed me he had not heard a thing. It was a little windy that day, but it was unusual for the turkey not to respond.

"It's like they just stopped talking and went silent," he said.

I agreed as I had heard them early that morning where my first spot had been, but they had just dropped off. Birds are strange.

The hubs started talking about walking again. *Sigh.*

I chose this life, I *chose* this life. I chose *this* life. I kept telling myself as my heels rubbed against the back of my boots, guaranteeing a quarter-sized blister for the next week.

"You know what? I'm going in."

"Yeah?" he said.

"Yeah, my dogs are barking, and I'm getting pretty tired."

"Okay, I will make my way back in a minute, do you mind grabbing the decoys?"

"No problem." I started to walk away.

"Do you know which way the pipeline is?" (The pipeline is a clearing that we used to walk in on this side of the property. It's like the main street.)

"That way, yes, that way." I pointed over my head to a general direction.

"Okay, see you back at the car."

Heading back, I had grabbed Larry and Louisa. They were heavy as they were made of a thick rubber cast in the shape of turkeys and were not a light load like Martha was.

About a quarter mile away from the car, I had had enough. I couldn't stand my boots any longer, and I knew it was mostly grass and dirt the rest of the way back. I took off my boots, tied my laces together, and threw them over my shoulder. I grabbed Larry and Louisa by their necks and made my way. Getting close to my car, I saw a red pickup parked about 100 feet from my car.

Who in the world was on our property! How did they get in? Don't they know trespassing is illegal!

The other family members who hunt out here only hunt during deer season, and they were all gone on an annual family trip!

I start to walk toward the pickup, seeing guys I did not know sitting as if they were waiting in the passenger and back seat. I didn't have my gun, and I had no boots on carrying two turkey decoys by their necks. I looked like a homeless hunter.

I walked up to the window where the passenger just stared at me.

My hair was messy and had a leaf hanging off my once perfect ponytail. I motioned for him to roll down his window.

"What's up?" I asked casually, hoping he could give me a reasonable answer to his presence.

"Not much," he said.

"What're you doin' out *here?*" I was ready to get to the bottom of it, and if I were to be attacked, I was throwing Larry at him.

He pointed back toward my car. "Casey will be back in a second."

Casey, my cousin, who has not gone on the spring trip in years. What a relief—for Larry.

"Oooh, good namedrop, buddy, I was getting worried there for a minute. Okay, thanks, y'all take care."

I walked away with my dirt-stained white socks standing out against the green grass and red dirt like camouflage pants at a black-tie affair.

Walking away from the red pickup toward my car, there was Casey.

"Hey, Casey!" I holler. "I was getting worried. I have never seen your new truck before."

"Yeah, I was wondering whose white SUV that was up there," he said.

He was checking out who was "trespassing" on the land as well.

After we exchanged brief information, we found out we had all been hunting at the same time. I had a sigh of relief and felt sorry for Casey, who had to get in his truck and explain to his friends who the wild woman of Borneo was with rat-nest hair and no shoes.

Once I explained what had happened to the Hubs when he had made his way back to the car, it all made sense. Even on the size acreage we were on, more than a couple of callers will confuse male turkeys to no end. They didn't know which "female" to go to hearing all those calls.

It's all about communication, isn't it? We were all trying to call these toms, and meanwhile, we didn't even think that there would be other people we would need to call to make sure our calls were worth calling. It was pure accident because none of us were aware the other would be out there, but now we are friends on FB to take care of such matters in the future.

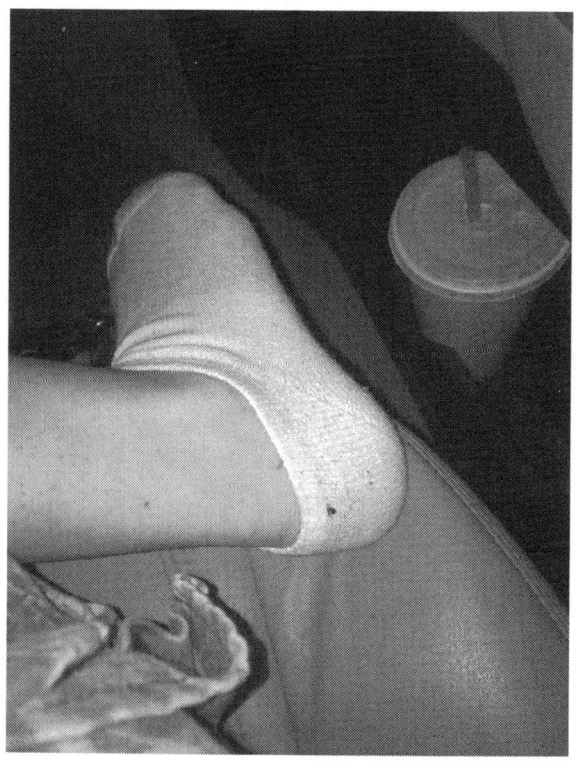

See that black spot on my sock? That is one of the four friends who migrated from the tick colony to me. I just wanted people to know they were returned to their maker and will never be heard from again!

Woman Up

The hubs and I celebrated our wedding anniversary last month.

But right before the actual day came about, we (I, for sure) were celebrating the fact that I would get to go hunting. I have not gone since 2012 due to having our youngest being born last year, and this would be the first time ever I would be by myself. Normally, I would just hang with the hubs and read or draw while he hunted.

This year was different.

The hubs and I went hunting a few times in November and early December. The first time was, "We are getting deer"—that was our mantra. By the third trip (which were all different weekends), our mantra had changed. It was now, "If we can put it in the freezer, shoot it!"

Sidenote: If you are sitting in a deer blind, which is just a tent with little windows that you can zip down to see out, birds hopping in the dead leaves sounds *exactly* like a deer!

The hubs was in a deer stand, which was about five miles from me. We were both shooting with rifles, and so we knew that if one of us were to shoot, the other could make their way toward the other one to help out.

Well, sure enough, after a couple of hours of my bird-watching and talking myself down from blasting an annoying bird with a rifle powerful enough to drop a deer, I heard it—*boom, boom!*

Two booms means either a) he missed (not likely as he seriously should test to have a marksman title), or b) there were two animals! Which would be strange because with deer, we only get as singles because most deer run like crazy after hearing a rifle shot and seeing their buddy on the ground.

So I got out of the blind and closed it up to walk to the road. Oh, and Papa was with us with his pickup, and he came to pick me up. He had been five miles in the other direction up the hill.

We started driving toward where the hubs was and saw him close to the road. Looking for his kill with excitement and anticipation, I saw no deer. It was starting to get dark, and so I was curious what happened as I knew we had no time to go back out to hunt longer. But then Papa said, "Look right there, on the ground. See the black?"

Kind of confused, I looked to where he was pointing, and sure enough, there was no deer. He had not killed a deer. He had not missed either. My husband was the good shot I thought him to be because lying before us were *two* black wild hogs.

Now, to explain wild hogs would be the same as explaining an illness that wipes out a population. These suckers are no joke. These are not cute pink Wilburs that you can house-train and make a pet for your family to enjoy. These are highly dangerous to the land, wildlife, and even people. They will take over because they breed at a ridiculous rate, and they tear up land in a way that would make any landowner scream. If you want to make a landowner happy, offer to hunt wild hogs off his land.

Since we were hunting on private land, we knew this was providing good fortune in two ways:

1. We had meat.
2. Two less hogs that the landowner and caretaker of this land would have to worry about.

But again, with any hunt, there comes a word that makes any wife smile and sigh at the same time—*processing*.

Now, my kitchen was spared at first because we were away from our home. Papa could help the hubs, and I could retreat to the warm house with Nana, where I could tell her about the hunt while the men processed the hogs.

I refuse to learn how to cut up any kill. It's not that it bothers me. The sight and mostly the smell I can handle. I just know how life works. If I learn how, then it might be expected of me to do it. Nope. We are a hunting family, and everyone has their part. I am in the packaging department, the washing department, the organizing-all-the-processing-gear department. I will not overqualify myself to know the cutting-up part because I might take away my husband's job, and I would never want to do that to him. I'm just that caring.

So the hogs were being hung up to cut up, and I made sure the guys had everything they needed in the way of supplies, and I retreated to the warm house to chat with Nana. After my hands and toes had their feeling and color back, I checked back with them for progress (like I would know what a "good" job looks like. I am not qualified to do so). Papa started to say he wasn't feeling well and he needed to go inside for a minute—not good.

There I stood, minding my distance, when the hubs said, "Need ya for a minute."

First of all, there is never *a* minute. You can guarantee twenty of those "minutes" for sure.

"Okay, what cha need?" I replied, instantly regretting I gave the impression I wanted to be a helper.

"Put both of your hands against the spine."

Huh? The hog's spine? Is the hog okay with this? Is he going to come alive even though you have his entire body rid of skin and two of the legs in the ice chest? Will it make noise like when we process chickens and it still has vocal cords intact and the chicken makes a huffing sound at your mom?

"With my hands?" I said, hoping he changed his mind.

"Yes, push with all your weight against it," he said with confidence.

He wasn't serious. He could not be serious. I liked bacon and pork chops, but this was seriously testing my love for pork.

Remembering my vows at that moment and repeating them to myself was all I could do. Why else would I do this? I was not qualified for this. He knew and loved the pitiful wimp I was when it came to these things. Surely he didn't want me to touch warm animal flesh with my bare hands in the cold of night. Didn't he know I had to pee?

"Okay," I said with the quietest breath I could manage.

I made fists to crack my knuckles, as if that was going to make this any easier. I raised my hands slowly to do as my husband asked.

I am an awesome wife. I am such an awesome, good, mentally scared wife.

I had to talk myself.

Pushing both my hands against the hog and leaning forward and putting my head down, as if I was stretching my calves, I cringed and squinted my eyes shut. My shoes were sliding in the mud as the hubs started working on the hog from the other side, pushing weight back against me. I tuned out everything I heard from the other side of this beast.

I am not qualified to do this. I am wearing a very nice ring that the man I love (who is working a knife with such skill on the other side of this mammoth and so sweetly asked me to do this) risked his life to buy for me. I shouldn't be doing this.

The hog carcass moved to the side, which I held on to with dear life as my feet slid around in the mud. Regaining my strength and footing, I kept talking to myself. *I am wearing items that were purchased at Victoria's Secret. I should not be doing this.*

"Keep pressing in, babe," my hunter said from the other side. *Babe*—cute. The movie started playing in my head of the precious little pig.

I am a buck fifteen soaking wet. I should not be doing this. Please, Lord above who is all loving and holy, take me now. Please come to this earth for the Second Coming so I may not have to be in this act of love a devotion any longer.

"All right, you're good."

Instantly pivoting on my cold, wet sneaker toe, I walked away from this scene of horror and feared I was a part of for all three and a half minutes. Wiggling my fingers and shaking my hands to shake off any goo this monster left on me, I took a breath and realized I survived. I didn't cry. I didn't squeal. I could handle this, I touched that thing and managed to live through it.

"Hey, babe?" the hubs called out from the blood fest.

Taking in a breath, I was ready to talk with people besides myself again. "Yeah?"

"Can you put the head of the hog in this bag for me?"

Dear Lord...

More Kids?

No, I am not pregnant.

But the thought, while I am still in my twenties, does go through my head. The hubs and I have these talks every once in a while, especially when we have talks of how the day went.

Some days I could say with a sweet smile that it was a four-kid day, which of course means I could see us having two more kids.

Some days—with a twitch in my eye, followed by a single tear—gritting my teeth, I'd manage to say it was a two-kid day, and one of us needs to go to the doctor to ensure that number!

So far, today has been a four-kid day. I don't know if it's because the radar for my image of four kids has been so real, but truthfully, I do not know if we are "done." We have talked about it, and the thought of four kids running around does not scare me. It's the first year that is the toughest for me. I know if we have a third, we will have a fourth. The hubs and I like things even, so we figured to make shopping for a dining-room table easy. We just need to make sure to stay shopping in the six-seater section (say that five times fast).

The career I would not have with four kids is the least of my worries. I thought I wanted a career because, you know, I went to college and all. I even graduated! However, getting into the real world, I realized I could care less about what job I had. The moola is really what pays the bills for me, literally. The gratification from the job is frivolous. I was doing a job to help my family and give them an easier day.

When work defined me and gave me my identification, it was cool. I could look at my day at work and say, "Look at what I did." Now that I am not in the field, I see little value in it for me. Just the same, I do not need more kids to see myself as better. If we were to have more kids, I would be thrilled. Scared, but thrilled.

If and/or when we have more kids, we will be crossing the threshold of untraditional. Looking at the stats of how many kids the average American family has, three seems to push the limits of many. However, parents who have four kids are more confident in their parenting! Either way, there are always thoughts rolling through my mind with kids as the topic of concern:

Three is too many!
Don't let the kids outnumber you!
Your numbers aren't even!
Are you going to stack the beds now?
Going to the grocery store means at least one will be out
    of the cart at all times!
Four means your car is just about full!
When does the oldest one go to work?
Why does peeing on yourself not bother you!
When do they start doing their own laundry?

What will be will be.
Seriously, when do they start doing their own laundry!

Where Did I Go?

So the term *losing yourself* tends to be attached to the new mom thing where a woman just doesn't quite seem like the woman she was before. Oftentimes this is a negative phrase because things aren't as they were before, and the way it was before was comfortable.

"She's let herself go."

"She's not herself anymore."

Now, I am in full approval of those who say, "The mom thing is not for me."

Thank you for being honest! I truly believe it's not in everyone's plan for life to have kids. I have an aunt who was hands down the funniest aunt. She was one who never had a desire to have kids. She had four stepchildren and countless grandkids. However, she was my and my sister's closest aunt. I am amazed how people who have no desire to have children will still have fun kids' stuff on their, radar as if their world revolved around kids. No shame in that game, folks. Awesome aunts go a long way in their loved ones' lives.

For those who have kids or who have desire to have kids, it's a sudden fall, isn't it? I mean, you have the buildup and expectations of kids, whether you carry them yourself or adopt, but it is like—*bam!*—spotlight on! You are on, and things are forever changed. They are there; and they are forever involved in your thoughts, your worries, your dinner plans, your sleep schedule (if you are lucky enough to have one).

It's when the newness wears off, and the visitors are gone. The meals stop coming in from friends and family. It stops being cute; it starts being real. The diapers, no sleep, just getting to sleep only to be awaken by the needs that seem to be ever changing. There's no time to take care of yourself the way you used to, and it makes you mad because you realize how valuable that was. And then you feel guilty because it's no one's fault. It's just that priorities have changed. You still want to do what you did before, but your life has changed to where there is another take-care-of item on the list, and it bumps off a lot of other items that were once on that list.

Once it seems like you are going to be okay and this new life will survive, even though you never went through training nor read a book that covered *everything*, you develop a routine. You start to see that it *is* possible to do this; it just requires some readjusting. You see, there is life to be lived, and now it has a deeper purpose. Your job is not only to keep the baby alive but to nurture, teach, and love that child. You are the first people they will meet, and you are the one who teaches the meaning of love, fun, sharing, caring, and the countless boundaries in life to protect them, not ruin their fun.

Losing the old me and wondering about the dreams I had prekids, or the goals, or even just the fun, leisure activities I used to look forward to that are not an option now (lying out in the sun, reading a book, leaving my laptop on the floor) aren't as easily enjoyed. They *are*, however, so much more valuable; and when I do get to enjoy them, I appreciate them as I had not once done. As our identity changes with this new role, *parent*, it also makes us feel as if we are so much more aware of our actions and why we do things the way we do things. It is nothing like we've ever known before, and it cannot be understood by those who are not there. It's one the place in life that is the most difficult and rewarding. Most rewards in life do not come without great sacrifice. I think about how I have been told *many* times that the rewards of parenting come much later in life, to see how your child has turned out. They may become an adult and will no longer be a "child," but amazingly, parents never stop being parents.

What Is the Point of This, God?

This is pointless. What is the big deal? I am doing nothing. I am making nothing of this time.

This is what I told myself many times during the last year and a half. I could not begin to see the point of why I was at home with my kids even though I knew without a doubt I was doing what I was supposed to be doing.

Before our second son was born, I prayed, "If you want me to stay home with our kids, God, I will. But my heart has been set on helping to provide in a financial way for a long time, so if my heart needs changing, change it. I would rather be focused on your plan for my family and with me not liking it at first because I know you have a bigger picture in mind than I do. I have one-hundred-year blinders on, and so if this is what I need to do, let me know."

He did.

I felt without a shadow of a doubt that I needed to stay home. I let my then boss/ friend know, who supported me, being a former SAHM herself, and said, "You will not regret it."

So fast-forward to having two in diapers and not being around people my age for a few days in a row, and I was really wondering, *Are you sure this is what You want me to do? You were not kidding, right? I do not see how I am helping. I do not see how anyone is gaining from this. I feel like I am messing my kids up. I feel like I am gaining no skills or anything out of this!*

God has a sense of humor. He also has a loving, grace-filled voice that speaks so sweetly, and sometimes He is silent and just lets a situation speak so loudly. He does not need to speak a word to get his point across.

Here are my life goals that I know cannot be accomplished overnight:

I want to be able to handle a stressful situation with ease and a smile.

I admire those women who seem to have straight chaos going on around them, and they have the attitude of *we got this, no need to stress.* And they are being truthful. They have no front going on. They *actually* see it that way, and they handle it with ease.

Well, God gave me two boys under two.

You want it? You got it, kiddo! Full immersion!

I found out not losing it is straight up self-control and patience. The only way to gain those bad boys is to live it out!

That is tough. I know for a fact that this means *many* times things are not going to go my way, and so it is go time for self-control with how I react to them. There is no blame game, as if to say, *Well, if they would have just done this, I would not have been mad and reacted that way.*

Yeah, like anyone would buy that for a minute. Put your big-girl panties on and have some accountability! You had an idea for life to go one way, and it went another. How many times did you try to take the same road and expect a different destination?

Okay, I got it.

Another life goal: Keep a home that is inviting and makes the people who enter feel welcomed and loved, whether they be family or not.

Well, if I can figure a system around little ones who don't quite understand why it's such a big deal to pour out buttermilk, tea, orange juice, or the 289,835th box of pasta on the kitchen floor, then I could possibly develop a system to make meals on a daily basis, be grateful when we do get to eat out, and appreciate the amount of money it takes to feed our family a good meal.

I am learning so much that I would have cast judgment before because I didn't appreciate those housewives with their crazy lives. I seriously had no clue because I hadn't walked a day in their shoes. I didn't understand the work, but now that I know the work, I have no problems telling others no when it comes to taking something else on because I am aware of how much my plate holds. I don't brush off dinner because I know it is not fun to run around trying to figure out what to make with one pound of beef, half a box of pasta, and a can of black-eyed peas from New Year's that we never ate.

It rubs off on your tough spots, humbles you, and forces to get your rear in gear; because no matter the day, the survival of your family (clothes, food, and shelter) tends to be at your control.

So often I have heard that the wife is the temperature gauge of the house. I never wanted to be whiney, throw a fit, and have the house all up in arms because Mom isn't happy. Never. I understand I will get mad, things will not go my way, and there will be seasons that life is tough. But how *I* deal with it is what will be noticed. *My* character will show, and *I* am the one who will need to answer for it. My husband and my kids will be a reflection of me. I don't want my husband to feel he has to walk on eggshells with me. I want to feel like he has the freedom to talk to me about whatever he wants and not have him trying to tread lightly because I am an emotional basket case who can't take uneasy subjects. I want my kids to have a laughing house. I want them to enjoy being home and to look back and say, "Yeah, life wasn't always easy, but we laughed through it."

All this being my goal means I have to work on many things to get there. I do wonder if me staying at home is God's way of letting me focus on all this. If I am in my home,

I can *see* my home. I can see how I react to the hardships with kids, dirty floors, and waking up to a load of laundry still in the washer from the night before—versus going to work to leave it all here and let it escape my memory for the day and not give it a second thought until I come back home, during which would be time to fix dinner, again.

This truly is a short job offer that will not be here forever. My kids will grow up. They will go to school, and one day, who knows, even move out. I will miss this mess one day. I will miss the quality time that they want to be around me. I will miss having a mess to clean up. Right now it's cool to see that God's point in all of this is that he gives me chances to serve my friends in their time of need. If I had been working, there would be no way I could watch my friend's three kids when she went into labor a month early. There would be no way for me to see where I needed improvement to get to that place of serving God and others with a gracious heart and not with a smiling mask.

The journey is long, but the rewards are wholesome. I want quality, which means consistency, which takes hard work. No quick fix, no shortcut. It's the road where, if I travel down with an open mind and a caring heart, I will begin to see how I am not where I should be, I am not where I want to be, but I am not where I was.

I like that plan.

Military Wife Life

I can't recall many books/movies of real-life heroes that I can relate to. I certainly cannot relate to Chris Kyle's life and story, but my husband can. I can, however, relate to his wife, sorta. Watching the movie, I did know about the ending and all, but I was surprised that the movie brought me to tears—oh, say about four times before the actual ending.

Background: My husband has served two tours overseas, both in Iraq. I didn't know this until after we saw the film, but he served at the same time as Chris Kyle (this gave me goose bumps). We saw the movie and then left the packed theater when the film ended and walked to the car. It was dark, and we got into the car out of the cold night air. I got my seat belt buckled, and neither of us had said a word since the movie ended. I took a deep breath because this movie had hit me hard emotionally; and as I lay my head back on the headrest, trying to hold back another round of tears, I heard the hubs's voice say the words from across the dark car, "Makes you want to go back down to the recruiter's office and sign back up."

The tears fell down my face. My eyes were closed, my nose was running—it was not a pretty cry.

I cannot express how much pride I have in my husband. We had not been dating two years before he was deployed the first time, and when he got the orders for his second deployment, we knew it would be tough. We were married by that time; so we knew right away we would be spending our first Thanksgiving, our first wedding anniversary, and our second Christmas away from each other.

When he came home the second time, we were so happy to be back together, but now was the hard part.

When you see the scenes of Chris coming home and he is physically with his family but obviously sidetracked, distracted—just not there although the smile is—it's tough. One reason is because the person whom you kiss good-bye to go overseas does not come home, not the same person anyway. You see them, and there is no button to press to "change" them back. What they just lived through is now a part of them forever.

The job for the wife is to be supportive, loving, caring, and just *there* for the one she loves. That part is easy; it's almost natural. The challenging part is when you no longer have the tools to do a job.

You are looking into the eyes of a person who is trying to cope with the fact that life has slowed down, their guard *can* come down (not likely to happen for a while), and they are allowed to have fun. The 180-miles-an-hour pace they have been going at for months has slowed to easy coasting. There is no forcing them to enjoy themselves. There is no forcing them to "let it out."

When a solider has been trained to do a job, that's just what they will do. The task will be performed. It will be completed, and whether that smile is real or not does not matter too much. When they see *you* are smiling, that is the tiny chipping away at that hard shell. So the fact that they are in "work mode" for some time after tends to be the shocker of the "reuniting" of the newlyweds.

This is heartbreaking and frustrating. You aren't mad at them; you are mad at the situation. You are mad because the person you love gave away pieces of themselves over there that were yours and your family's to enjoy—not for someone who wants to kill them, throw them into the sand, and stomp on them. You are heartbroken because you want to scream that the person you are dedicated to has *given* a level of dedication to his country. So many in his country want to complain and whine because they may feel upset about something going differently from how they feel it should go, and yet they sit on our free soil with the freedom to complain because your loved one just got back defending that freedom.

As you are on the phone or chatting with him overseas, the screen shakes on his side, and there is a boom. He pauses and then says, "Hold on. I need to check my laundry."

He comes back with a forced smile on his face, acting as though nothing just happened, and you know the drill of going along with it because nothing can be said at that time.

Two days later, you find out that him checking his laundry was actually a building next door getting bombed; and a shrapnel from what once was a toilet had flown into the building where your loved one sleeps. Great.

Many moments in the movie are sad, but some are truly inspiring. I thought it was great to see how Chris Kyle enjoyed going to the VA to help other vets who were injured or had lost a limb in combat. The therapy that veterans can truly only give to other vets is priceless. They have been there, literally, and to think about the way they are able to give a knowing look as they talk with one another is encouraging.

Props to Clint Eastwood. He made a war movie that did not glamorize war. He got to the real issues with military couples. He didn't go for what would sell because—let's face it—there has been a few war movies made in our time. And thankfully, he stuck to a *real* story with *real* people. He showed how gross it can be overseas.

I remember many times the hubs would tell me it did smell over there. It was hot, and it smelled horribly. It has a depressing feeling because no matter what sense you are turning to for some relief, there is a feeling of misery in the air.

There is a certain level of anger that anyone watching the film might feel at the end when they see that Chris was taken by a fellow vet. It was when he let his guard down that his life ended. I know this is easy to see, but my heart breaks for his children and his wife. They so wanted to have him home to get time back that they had lost while he was overseas fighting. I think that is one of the reasons Clint did not have to try to build this movie up. This true story was so appealing to those who have read the book and seen the movie because it has such dramatic details to the story that are like those of real life. Chris had bounties on his head that were creeping into dollar amounts so high Chris Kyle himself said jokingly he was scared his wife might turn him in. He had set records with his kills while being a hero to his wife and kids. No rewrites needed.

I hoped to read the book soon and, when I had, found many times that I enjoy the book because it does not have the time restraints that the film does. But I like seeing the film first because it gives me a visual of the setting and the people within the story.

Our friend, who is a Marine recruiter, said the film has inspired many eighteen-year-olds to come into the recruiting office ready to be a Chris Kyle. Our friend, who has a few tours under his belt, lays out the realities of this career. He will not sugarcoat it to get his numbers. He lets them know—as best as one can in a comfortable office setting—that there is a reason for the word *sacrifice* being associated with this career choice. You never know how much it will take.

Ode to the Working Mom

During this writing, the strangest thing happened to me.

I was offered a job.

Really strange. Was not looking for it. Tried to turn it down. I did one thing though. I had plateaued with my "staying home" ways.

Here's what happened.

My husband and I have been wanting for some time to send our oldest and youngest, when the time came, to a school here in town. It's a Christian school, and we knew their three-year-old program was going to be taking application soon. I decided one day when the boys were at Mother's Day Out to take a tour of this school. The principal happened to give me a tour and was very nice. My good friend, whose boys also attended this school, was there that day filling in for the secretary. She gave me a quick wave and a smile as I started my tour. It was a nice school, bright and fun. Artwork and newest writings were displayed in the hallways, and every so often when I would peek in a classroom, I would see kids and teachers going on with their daily routine.

After the tour had ended, the principal and I were standing in the office where we were talking about tuition and other mom questions. Amid the conversation, he casually asked, "So do you work?"

"I stay at home with my boys," I respond with a peace and comfort about myself.

"Do you want to work?" he responds.

"No, I'm good with staying home."

God was no doubt in heaven rubbing his hands together in preparation for the next twenty-four hours—wearing a grin and bright light, fixing to rock my *comfortable* world.

I thanked the principal as I walked out, giving a quick hug to my friend who was sitting at the desk asking me how I liked the school. We chatted for a minute, and then I headed out to get the boys.

Twenty minutes later, my good friend is asking me through a text why I told him I didn't want to work.

Do you have that friend who, with the upmost care and love, can text you and get your attention faster than chocolate-covered strawberries? Well, that is my friend T. T is the best about telling me to get my rear in gear, and I know from her heart she is caring and only wants good in the outcome.

"Why does it matter?" I texted back.

"He was wanting to offer you a job!"

Say what? I was stunned, shocked, in disbelief. I had no words, only tears.

Through many prayers, asking God if this was really right, and making a checklist of questions knowing I would refuse the job if any of the answers were no.

They were all yes.

Okay, I get it. It was *God's* timing, not mine. It was his plan, and if I were to follow, I needed to follow and stop being so stubborn.

So once the job had been confirmed and I was officially scared, the very kind principal and vice principal offered me a two-week observing time to get to know the school and basically get in touch with the teaching process within the second grade.

I had seen the grass on the other side of the fence. My dear Lord above. I had not worked full-time with two kids. Ever. I was now staring at the realization that I was to get up, get myself *and* the kids ready, drop them off, and be at a certain place, on time I might add, every day for two whole weeks. You wanna talk about changing up the coffee routine?

Good granny, it was different. Oh, get this, after the full day (which was completely fun and relaxing. Not a stress at the school, the kids, and literally, everyone was so pleasant and kind), there is still dinner to think of! The hubs deserves so many gold medals for his role in this area! What a trooper. The man can cook.

To those working moms who want to sit for a minute after getting home from work to get off your feet for a few minutes, I raise my coffee to you.

To those working moms who have had that day and make the impromptu stop to pick up pizzas for dinner, I raise my iced coffee to you.

To those teachers who have been struggling with twenty students on that one concept that they are just not quite grasping all day, who then has to come home and realize that their own child is in need of speech therapy and wonder if the insurance will cover it, when also realizing that the mortgage has still not been mailed yet because she forgot the day before because she was up late preparing brownies for the next day. Just chew on the coffee grounds, girl.

I raise my cup to you, and you, and you. Bless you, my sisters. The days are long, but the years are short. May our stresses and worries be the thread in the blanket of wisdom and patience. May we thank the Lord for *our* lot and see the blessings among the stresses.

Made in the USA
Lexington, KY
14 June 2016